First English Words

Aprenda Inglês com Daisy, Ben e Keekee!

HarperCollins Publishers

Westerhill Road
Bishopbriggs
Glasgow
G64 2QT

First edition 2012

10 9 8 7 6 5 4 3

© HarperCollins Publishers 2012

ISBN 978-0-00-746714-3

Collins ® is a registered trademark of
HarperCollins Publishers Limited

www.collinslanguage.com

A catalogue record for this book is available
from the British Library

Printed by RR Donnelley APS

Artwork and design by Q2AMedia

Music and lyrics by Iskra Anguelova

Songs arranged and produced by
www.tomdickanddebbie.com

Additional typesetting by
Davidson Publishing Solutions, Glasgow

For the publisher:
Lucy Cooper   Kerry Ferguson   Elaine Higgleton
Kate Nicholson   Lisa Sutherland   John Whitlam

**Content developed and compiled by
Karen Jamieson**

This book includes a CD of songs and vocabulary. The tracks on the CD are:

1. Say the alphabet!
2. Song: I can count!
3. Words: I can count!
4. Song: Colour fun
5. Words: Colour fun
6. Song: Shape search
7. Words: Shape search.
8. Song: My body and face
9. Words: My body and face
10. Song: How I feel
11. Words: How I feel
12. Song: My family at home
13. Words: My family at home
14. Song: Things I do
15. Words: Things I do
16. Song: More things I do
17. Words: More things I do
18. Song: What's it like?
19. Words: What's it like?
20. Song: My day
21. Words: My day
22. Song: Playtime
23. Words: Playtime
24. Song: My classroom
25. Words: My classroom

26. Song: Art time
27. Words: Art time
28. Song: Music time
29. Words: Music time
30. Song: My bedtime
31. Words: My bedtime
32. Song: The fruit stall
33. Words: The fruit stall
34. Song: Supermarket visit
35. Words: Supermarket visit
36. Song: Breakfast time
37. Words: Breakfast time
38. Song: Lunchtime
39. Words: Lunchtime
40. Song: A special dinner
41. Words: A special dinner
42. Song: Baking day
43. Words: Baking day
44. Song: My birthday party
45. Words: My birthday party
46. Song: My pets
47. Words: My pets
48. Song: On the farm
49. Words: On the farm
50. Song: Safari sports day

51. Words: Safari sports day
52. Song: Jungle soccer
53. Words: Jungle soccer
54. Song: In the sea
55. Words: In the sea
56. Song: Rock pool band
57. Words: Rock pool band
58. Song: Bugs and mini-beasts
59. Words: Bugs and mini-beasts
60. Song: The weather
61. Words: The weather
62. Song: Summer clothes
63. Words: Summer clothes
64. Song: Winter clothes
65. Words: Winter clothes
66. Song: My town
67. Words: My town
68. Song: My house and garden
69. Words: My house and garden
70. Song: In the park with grandpa
71. Words: In the park with grandpa
72. Song: Fairytale castle
73. Words: Fairytale castle

Contents

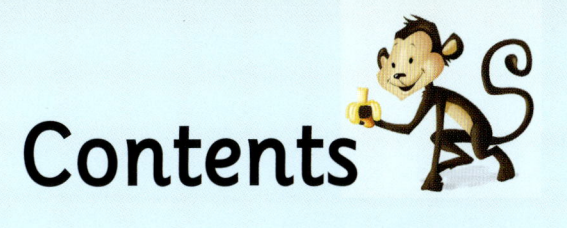

The alphabet

Aa

Bb

Cc

Dd

Ee

Ff

Gg

Hh

Ii

Jj

Kk

Ll

Mm

Nn

Oo

Pp

Qq

Rr

Ss

Tt

Uu

Vv

Ww

Xx

Yy

Zz

I can count!

1 one
uma

2 two
dois

3 three
três

4 four
quatro

5 five
cinco

Activities

1. Can you count to 10?
2. Sing the song!

Song

1, 2, 3, 4, 5
1, 2, 3, 4, 5

6 six *seis*

7 seven *sete*

8 eight *oito*

9 nine *nove*

10 ten *dez*

I can count, I can count,
I can count to five!

6, 7, 8, 9, 10
6, 7, 8, 9, 10

Can you count? Can you count,
Can you count to ten? YES!

Colour fun

white — branco

blue azul

green verde

Activities

1. Find the hidden snake.
2. Sing the song!

Song

Yellow and blue (x4)
make the green of the trees. (x2)

black
preto

purple
roxo

red
vermelho

orange
laranja

yellow
amarelo

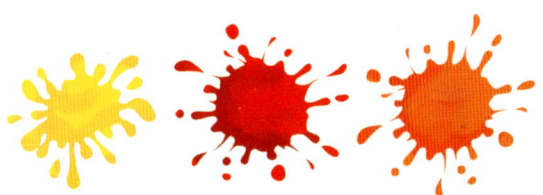

Yellow and red (x4)
make the orange of the sun. (x2)

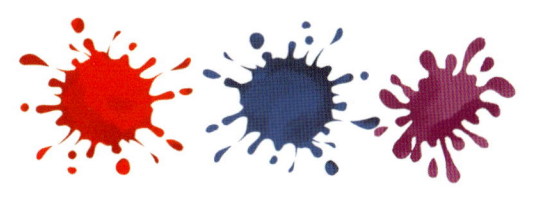

Red and blue (x4)
make the purple of the grapes. (x2)

Shape search

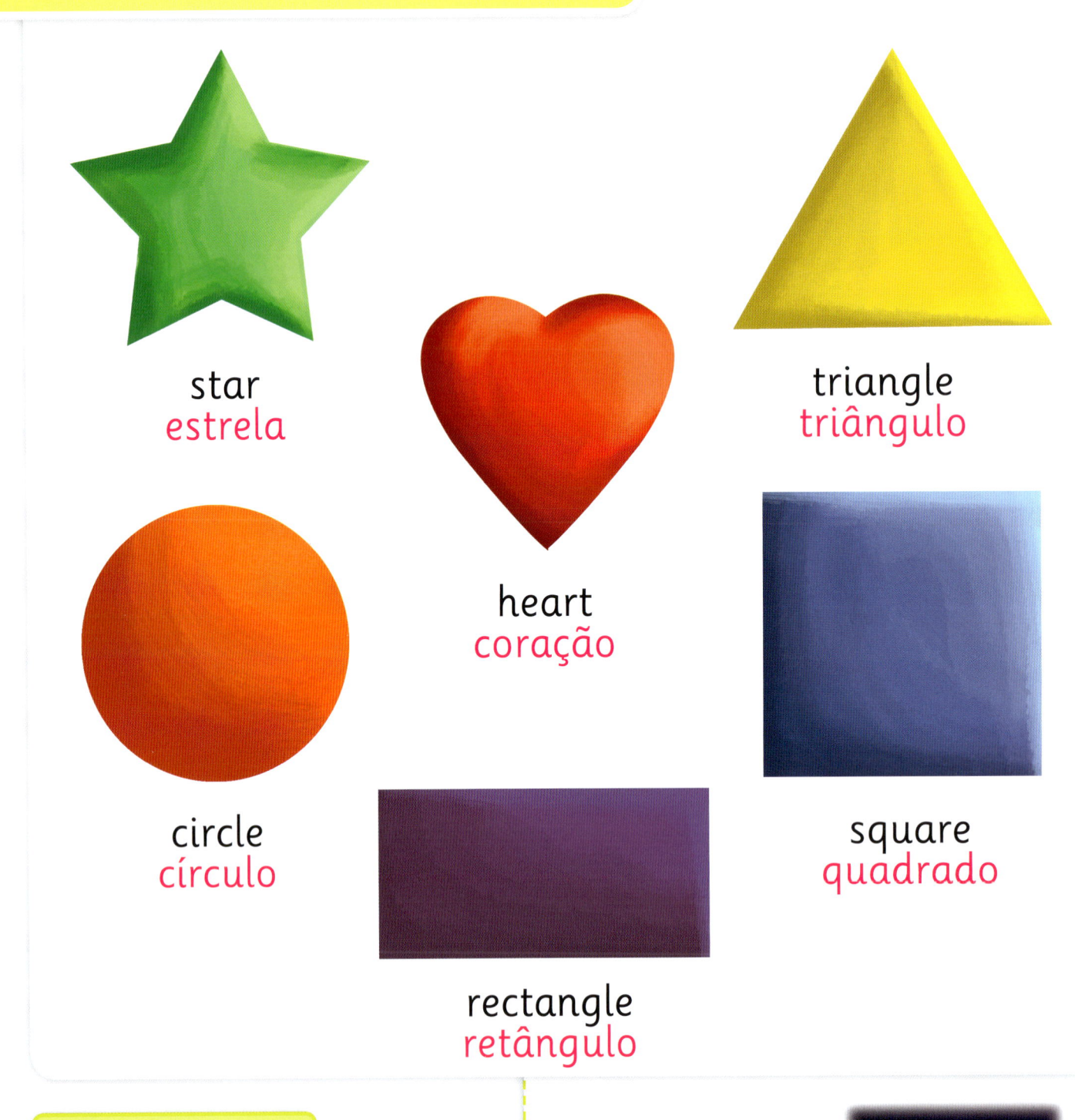

star
estrela

heart
coração

triangle
triângulo

circle
círculo

rectangle
retângulo

square
quadrado

Activities

1. Find the hidden mouse.
2. Sing the song!

Song

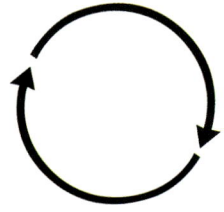

Round and round the circle goes.
The star shines in the sky.

Count the shapes

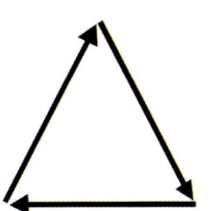

Three sides make a triangle.
A heart says 'I love you'.

The square is
like a window.

The rectangle's
like a door. (x2)

9

My body and face

head
cabeça

arm
braço

hand
mão

leg
perna

stomach
barriga

foot
pé

Activities

1. Find the hidden elephant.
2. Sing the song!

Song

One nose,

One mouth,

hair
cabelo

nose
nariz

eye
olho

ear
orelha

mouth
boca

Two eyes,

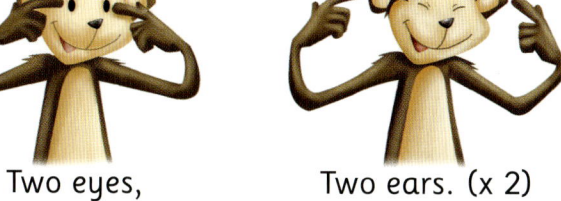

Two ears. (x 2)

Hair, hair, hair
everywhere!

Hair, hair, hair
everywhere!

How I feel

angry
com raiva

sad
triste

happy
feliz

tired
cansada

Activities

1. Find the hidden apple.
2. Sing the song!

Song

I am hungry. (x 2)
Hamburgers, fries!

hungry
com fome

thirsty
com sede

scared
com medo

shy
tímida

I am thirsty. (x 2)
Pour me some milk!

I am happy. (x 2)
Cuddle my cat!

I am tired. (x 2)
Let's go to bed!

My family at home

grandma
vovó

grandpa
vovô

Activities

1. Find the hidden parrot.
2. Who lives with you?
3. Sing the song!

Song

Look at mummy! Look at daddy!

daddy
papai

brother
irmão

mummy
mamãe

me!
eu!

sister
irmã

There's my sister,
baby brother.

Look at grandma! Look
at grandpa! Look at me!

This is my family!

Things I do

stand up
levantar

sit down
sentar

touch my toes
tocar a ponta dos pés

jump
pular

Activities

1. Find the hidden teddy.
2. Sing the song!

Song

Sit down, Daisy,
drink some juice. (x 2)
Sit down Daisy.

eat
comer

drink
beber

cry
chorar

laugh
rir

Stand up Ben, and
eat some grapes. (x 2)
Stand up, Ben.

Jump up, high,
then touch your toes. (x 2)
Jump up, Keekee.

Don't cry, Daisy!
Laugh with Ben. (x 2)
Don't cry, Daisy!

More things I do

hold hands
andar de mãos dadas

wave
dar tchau

run
correr

walk
andar

Activities

1. Find the hidden shell.
2. Sing the song!

Song

Let's make a circle! (x 2)
All hold hands! (x 2)

clap
bater palmas

turn around
dar voltas

rub my tummy
esfregar a barriga

make a circle
fazer uma roda

Turn around! (x 2)
Clap your hands! (x 2)

Here is your mummy! (x 2)
Run, run, run! (x 2)

Here is your mummy! (x 2)
Run, run, run! (x 2) Run!

What's it like?

slow
lenta

fast
rápida

small
pequeno

big
grande

Activities

1. Find the hidden train.
2. Sing the song!

Song

The rabbit is fast and
the turtle is slow.

20

strong
forte

weak
fraco

dirty
sujo

clean
limpo

The elephant's strong and the baby's weak.

The monkey's small, the gorilla's big!

Dirty hippo! Dirty hippo! Wash it clean!

21

My day

time to get dressed
hora de me vestir

time to get up
hora de levantar

time for school
**hora de ir
para a escola**

playtime
hora de brincar

snack time
hora do lanche

Activities

1. Find the hidden kangaroo.
2. Sing the song!

Song

Good morning! Good morning!
It's time to get up! (x 2)

story time
hora da história

home time
hora de voltar para casa

bath time
hora do banho

bedtime
hora de dormir

The school bell is ringing!
It's time for school! (x 2)

The water is lovely!
It's bath time, it's bath time! (x 2)

Good night! Good night!
It's bedtime! It's bedtime! (x 2)

Playtime

plane
avião

ball
bola

puzzle
quebra-
cabeça

blocks
blocos

Activities

1. Find the hidden duck.
2. What is your favourite toy?
3. Sing the song!

Song

What's in the toy box?
(x 2)

toy box
caixa de brinquedos

doll
boneca

panda bear
ursinho panda

train
trenzinho

fire engine
carro de bombeiros

rocket
foguete

Doll, panda bear, train.

Rocket and ball, puzzle and plane,

doll, panda bear, train. (x 2)

My classroom

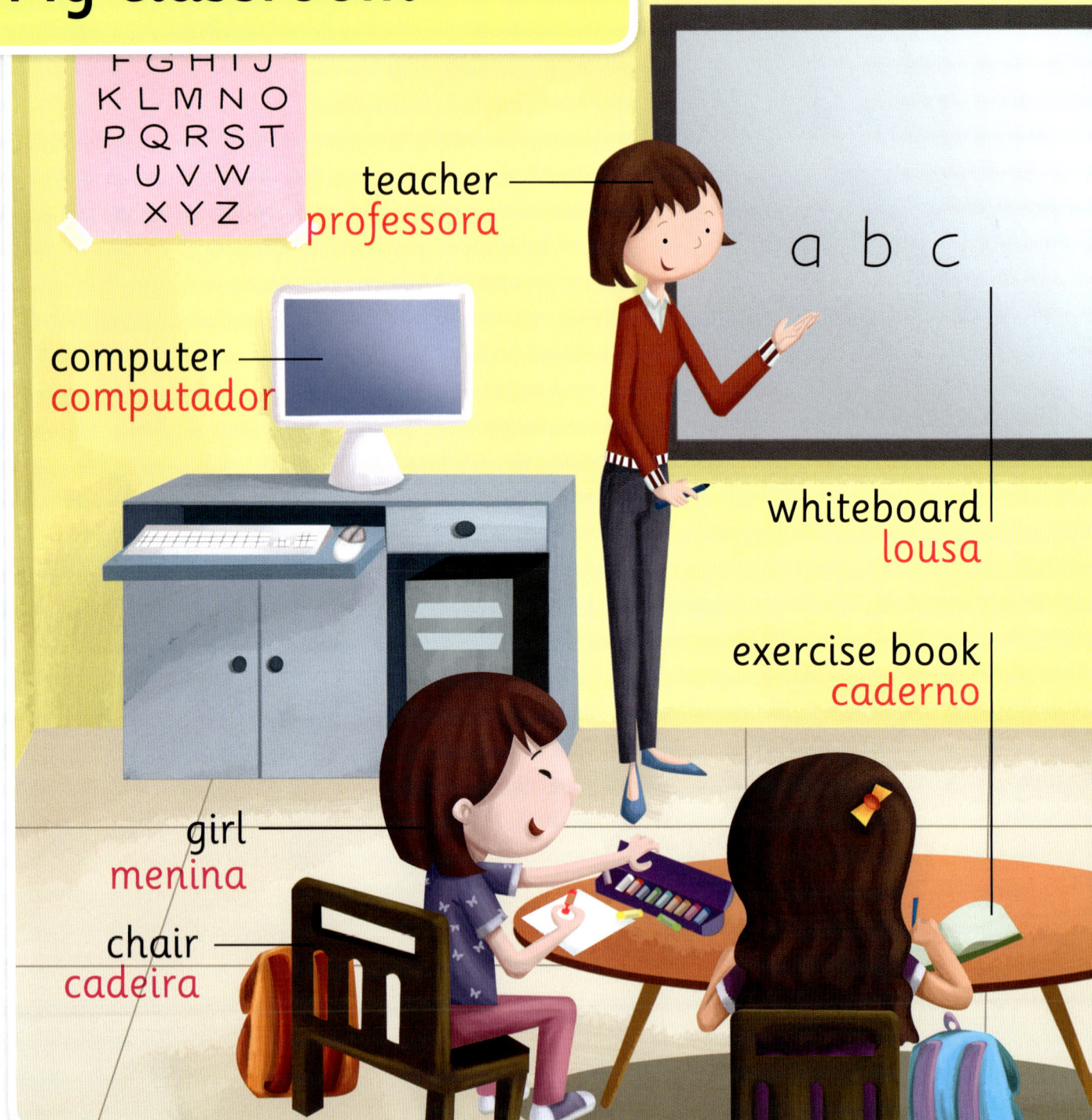

FGHIJ
KLMNO
PQRST
UVW
XYZ

teacher
professora

computer
computador

whiteboard
lousa

a b c

exercise book
caderno

girl
menina

chair
cadeira

Activities

1. Find the hidden birthday cake.
2. Sing the song!

Song

Girls and boys, girls and boys,

toys
brinquedos

boy
menino

table
mesa

books
livros

bag
mochila

sit on your chairs!

Open your books! (x 2)

Look at the teacher,
at the whiteboard! (x 4)

Art time

paper
papel

crayons
giz de cera

glue
cola

scissors
tesoura

Activities

1. Find the hidden rabbit.
2. Sing the song!

Song

Paper and crayons, markers and brush.
We're painting pictures. This is art class!

28

marker
marcador

pencils
lápis

brush
pincel

paint
tinta

Keekee is drawing. Ben's painting, too.
Daisy is pasting a star with some glue.

Paper and crayons, markers and brush.
We're painting pictures. This is art time!

Music time

keyboard
teclado

triangle
triângulo

trumpet
trompete

drum
tambor

Activities

1. Find the hidden pair of scissors.
2. Sing the song!

Song

Let's play music! (x 2)
The violin and xylophone,
the triangle and drum! (x 2)

violin
violino

xylophone
xilofone

guitar
guitarra

tambourine
pandeiro

Drum, drum, Keekee, play the drum!

Daisy plays the trumpet! Ben - the tambourine! (x 2)

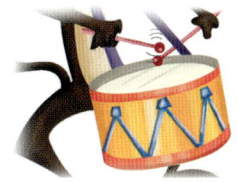

Drum, drum, Keekee, play the drum!

My bedtime

1. have a shower
tomar banho

2. dry myself
me enxugar

3. put on my pyjamas
pôr o pijama

4. brush my teeth
escovar os dentes

5. brush my hair
escovar o cabelo

Activities

1. Find the hidden cat.
2. Sing the song!

Song

At the end of the day,
I put on my pyjamas,
brush my teeth, brush my hair.

6. go to the toilet
ir ao banheiro

7. wash my hands
lavar as mãos

8. get into bed
deitar na cama

9. cuddle my teddy
abraçar meu ursinho

10. kiss goodnight
dar um beijo de boa-noite

At the end of the day,
I get into bed, cuddle my teddy
and kiss him goodnight.

Kiss my mummy,
say goodnight.
(x 2)

At the end of the day,
I get into bed, cuddle my teddy
and say goodnight!

The fruit stall

watermelons
melancias

pears
peras

strawberries
morangos

pineapples
abacaxis

oranges
laranjas

Activities

1. Find the hidden seahorse.
2. What is your favourite fruit?
3. Sing the song!

Song

I like peaches,
I like pears.

grapes
uvas

cherries
cerejas

peaches
pêssegos

apples
maçãs

bananas
bananas

Keekee likes
bananas. (x 2)

Watermelon,
apples, grapes,

oranges and cherries!
(x 2)

Supermarket visit

lettuces
alfaces

mushrooms
cogumelos

carrots
cenouras

cucumbers
pepinos

red peppers
pimentões vermelhos

Activities

1. Find the hidden train.
2. Which vegetables do you like best?
3. Sing the song!

Song

Daddy's got a
basket. (x 2)

broccoli
brócolis

green peppers
pimentões verdes

potatoes
batatas

onions
cebolas

tomatoes
tomates

basket
cestinha

Carrots, lettuce, mushrooms, onions, broccoli.

Daddy's got a basket. (x 2)

Carrots, lettuce, mushrooms, onions, broccoli.

Breakfast time

toast
torradas

tea
chá

yoghurt
iogurte

cup
xícara

Activities

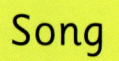

1. Find the hidden paintbrush.
2. What do you have for breakfast?
3. Sing the song!

Song

Milk and cereal, bread and jam,
Daisy likes to eat. (x 2)

coffee
café

cereal
cereal

milk
leite

juice
suco

spoon
colher

honey
mel

bread
pão

jam
geleia

Mummy, mummy, pass me the honey!
Daddy, daddy, give me the toast!

Milk and cereal, bread and jam,
Daisy likes to eat.

Lunchtime

sushi
sushi

chocolate
chocolate

chicken
frango

egg rolls
rolinhos primavera

noodles
miojo

tacos
tacos

At school

Activities

1. Find the hidden flower.
2. What's your favourite food?
3. Sing the song!

Song

I am hungry! I am hungry
– some pizza, please!

cheese
queijo

salad
salada

meat sauce
molho de carne

pizza
pizza

corn
milho

pasta
macarrão

At home

Mummy, pass me, mummy,
pass me, salad and corn!

Noodles, tacos, chicken,
sushi, chocolate and cheese!

I am hungry, I am hungry!
It's time for lunch.

A special dinner

steak
bife

peas
ervilha

fork
garfo

knife
faca

rice
arroz

fish
peixe

ketchup
ketchup

Activities

1. Find the hidden flower.
2. Sing the song!

Song

Rice and fish,
steak and peas,

fries
batata frita

hamburger
hambúrguer

soup
sopa

baked potato
batata assada

beans
feijão

I'm so hungry, give me some, please! (x 2)

Hamburger, fries, baked potatoes, beans

I'm so hungry, give me some, please! (x 2)

Baking day

butter
manteiga

syrup
melaço

flour
farinha

plate
prato

Activities

1. Find the hidden sunglasses.
2. Sing the song!

Song

Mummy's baking cookies.

cookies
biscoitos

oven
forno

bowl
tigela

sugar
açúcar

eggs
ovos

Daisy's cracking eggs.

Butter, flour, syrup.

This is baking day.

My birthday party

birthday present
presente de aniversário

ice cream
sorvete

birthday card
cartão de aniversário

Activities

1. Find the hidden bee.
2. Can you count the candles on the cake?
3. Sing the song!

Song

Are you ready for the party? (x 2)

Presents, cards, balloons! (x 3)

balloons
balões

popcorn
pipoca

sandwiches
sanduíches

cake
bolo

water
água

fruit
frutas

sweets
balas

Cake and sweets and popcorn, too!

Ice cream, water, fruit! (x 2)

Are you ready for the party? (x 2)

Presents, cards, balloons! (x 3)

My pets

dog
cachorro

puppy
cachorrinho

hamster
hamster

guinea-pig
porquinho-da-índia

Activities

1. Find the hidden umbrella.
2. Can you hop like a rabbit and stretch like a cat?
3. Sing the song!

Song

Ben and Daisy have some pets: cat, dog, rabbit. (x 2)

cat
gato

kitten
gatinho

rabbit
coelho

tortoise
tartaruga

Puppy, hamster, guinea pig! (x 2)

Ben and Daisy have some pets:
cat, dog, rabbit!

On the farm

chicken
galinha

donkey
jumento

goose
gansa

duck
pata

Activities

1. Find the hidden octopus.
2. Can you make farm animal noises?
3. Sing the song!

Song

The goose and the duck (x 2)
live on the farm, on the farm.

cow
vaca

horse
cavalo

rat
rato

mouse
camundongo

sheep
ovelha

The cow and the horse (x 2)
live on the farm as well.

Donkey, chicken,
sheep and mouse
play along with them.

The cow and the horse (x 2)
live on the farm, on the farm.

51

Safari sports day

crocodile
crocodilo

giraffe
girafa

baboon
babuíno

cheetah
guepardo

zebra
zebra

Activities

1. Find the hidden hat.
2. Sing the song!

Song

The cheetah and the zebra,
the hippo and the rhino.

52

lion
leão

elephant
elefante

hippo
hipopótamo

rhino
rinoceronte

Run, run, running down
the road! (x 2)

The lion's jumping over the stick!
Jump! Jump! Jump! Jump! (x 2)

Jungle soccer

snake
cobra

gorilla
gorila

tiger
tigre

monkey
macaco

chimpanzee
chimpanzé

Activities

1. Find the hidden drum.
2. Sing the song!

Song

Jungle soccer is
the game

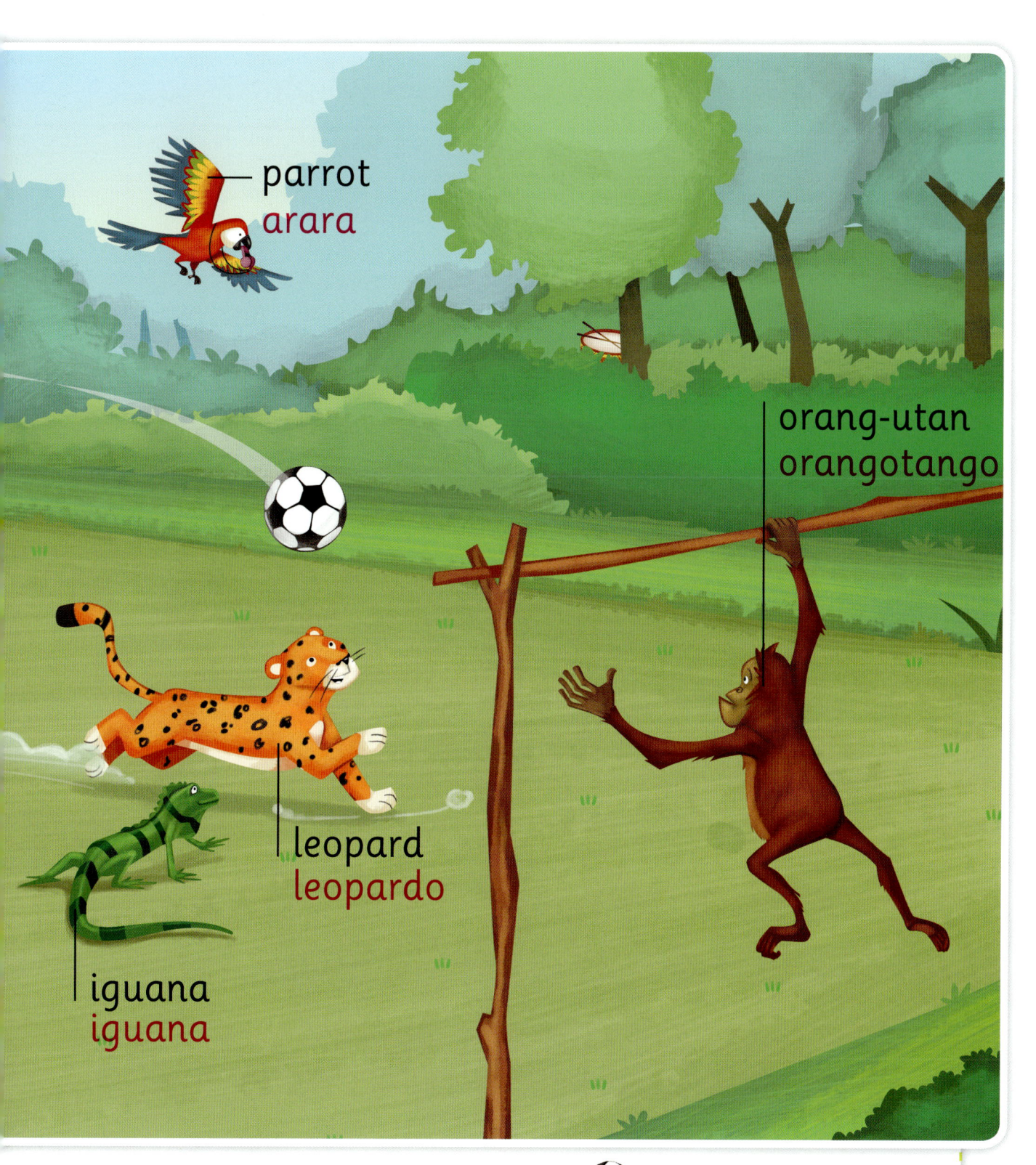

parrot
arara

orang-utan
orangotango

leopard
leopardo

iguana
iguana

gorillas and orang-utans
like to play! (x 2)

Monkeys, tigers
and chimpanzees,

kick the ball and play
with me! (x 2)

In the sea

dolphin
golfinho

shark
tubarão

seal
foca

octopus
polvo

shipwreck
navio naufragado

Activities

1. Find the hidden school bag.
2. Sing the song!

Song

In the sea, in the sea
lives a dolphin.

walrus
morsa

whale
baleia

penguin
pinguim

turtle
tartaruga

In the sea, in the sea
live his friends.

The octopus, the penguin,
the seal and the turtle,

all live in the sea! (x 2)

Rock pool band

jellyfish
água-viva

starfish
estrela-do-mar

rock
rocha

shell
concha

Activities

1. Find the hidden spoon.
2. Sing the song!

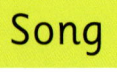

Song

Jellyfish, jellyfish,
play the drums!

seahorse
cavalo-marinho

fish
peixe

crab
caranguejo

seaweed
algas

Starfish, seahorse
sing a song!

Jellyfish, jellyfish,
play the drums!

Seaweed, crab,
join the rock pool band!

Bugs and mini-beasts

butterfly
borboleta

bee
abelha

beetle
besouro

ladybird
joaninha

Activities

1. Find the hidden bananas.
2. Sing the song!

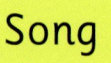

Song

Fly, fly, butterfly,

60

caterpillar
lagarta

spider
aranha

ant
formiga

cricket
grilo

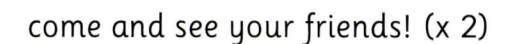

come and see your friends! (x 2)

The little bee, the ladybird,
the caterpillar, ant! (x 2)

The weather

rainy
chuvoso

snowy
nevado

sunny
ensolarado

windy
ventoso

Activities

1. Find the hidden tiger.
2. Colour a weather picture.
3. Sing the song!

Song

Open the umbrella!
It's rainy, it's rainy!
Open the umbrella!
It's rainy today!

cloudy
nublado

hot
quente

cold
frio

stormy
tempestuoso

How the snow is falling!
It's snowy, it's snowy!
How the snow is falling!
It's snowy today!

Look the kite is flying!
It's windy, it's windy!
Look the kite is flying!
It's windy today!

How the sun is shining!
It's sunny, it's sunny!
How the sun is shining!
It's sunny today!

Summer clothes

skirt
saia

T-shirt
camiseta

swimming
trunks
calção
de banho

swimsuit
maiô

Activities

1. Find the hidden trumpet.
2. Sing the song!

Song

Sunglasses, sun hat,
sandals and skirt! (x 2)

shirt
camisa

sunglasses
óculos
de sol

sun hat
chapéu de sol

shorts
bermuda

dress
vestido

sandals
sandália

Swimming trunks and swimsuit,
T-shirt and shorts (x 2)

Summer time! Summer time!
Summer time is here! (x 2)

Winter clothes

jacket
jaqueta

trousers
calça

boots
bota

coat
casaco

Activities

1. Find the hidden bicycle.
2. Sing the song!

Song

Mummy's wearing boots.

gloves
luva

hat
gorro

scarf
cachecol

sweatshirt
blusa de
moletom

shoes
sapato

jeans
jeans

Daisy's wearing gloves.

Ben is wearing jeans,
shoes and a hat.

Winter time is here!
(x 3)

My town

swimming pool
piscina

hairdresser
cabeleireiro

library
biblioteca

school
escola

bus
ônibus

motorbike
moto

bike
bicicleta

Activities

1. Find the hidden chimpanzee.
2. Which of these things have you seen in your town?
3. Sing the song!

Song

The swimming pool and hairdresser,

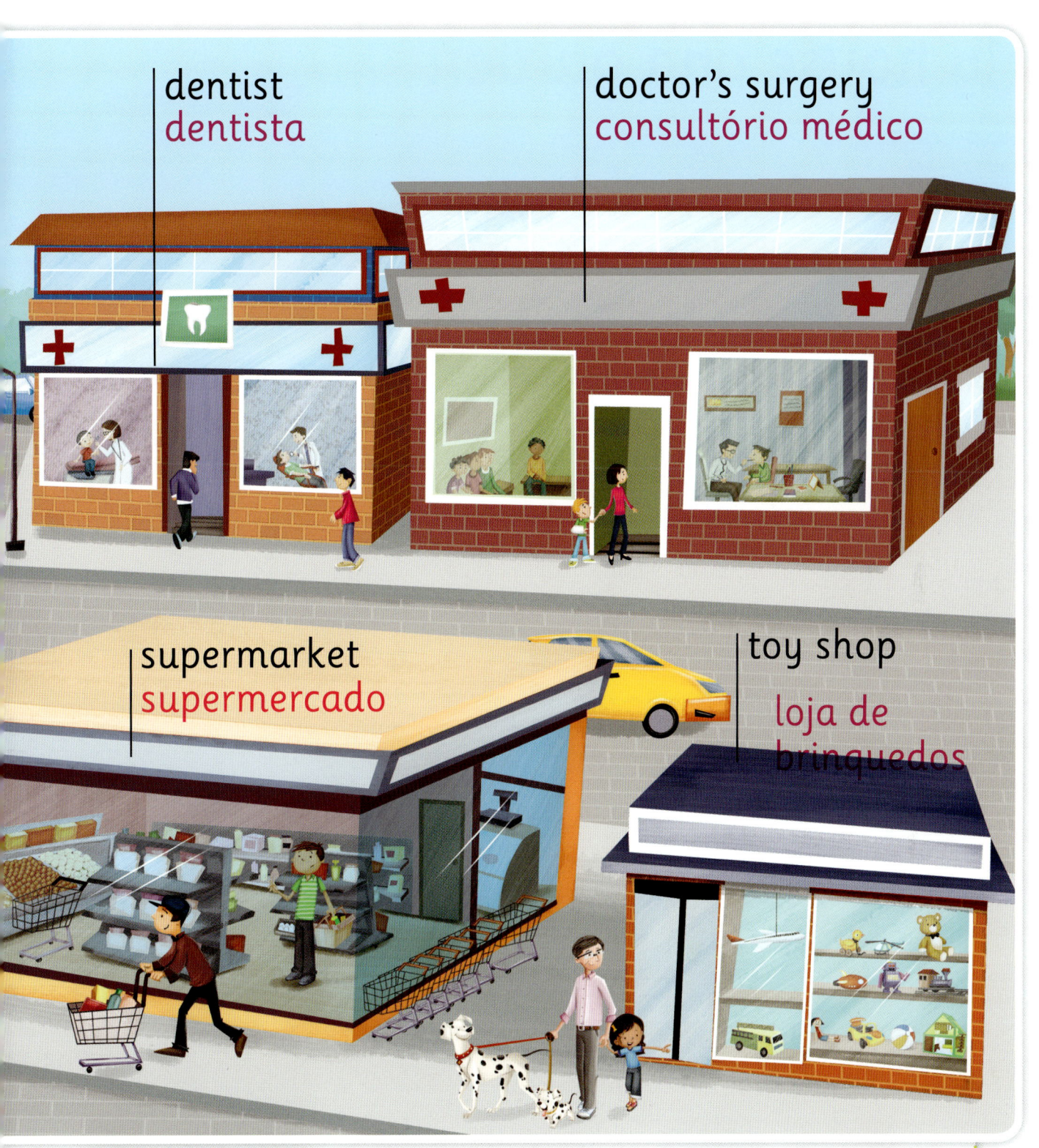

dentist
dentista

doctor's surgery
consultório médico

supermarket
supermercado

toy shop
loja de brinquedos

library and school.
(x 2)

Take the bus!
Ride a bike! (x 2)

To the swimming pool and
hairdresser, library and school.

My house and garden

tree
árvore

window
janela

flower
flor

garden
jardim

Activities

1. Find the hidden guitar.
2. Sing the song!

Song

Open the window!
Close the door! (x 2)

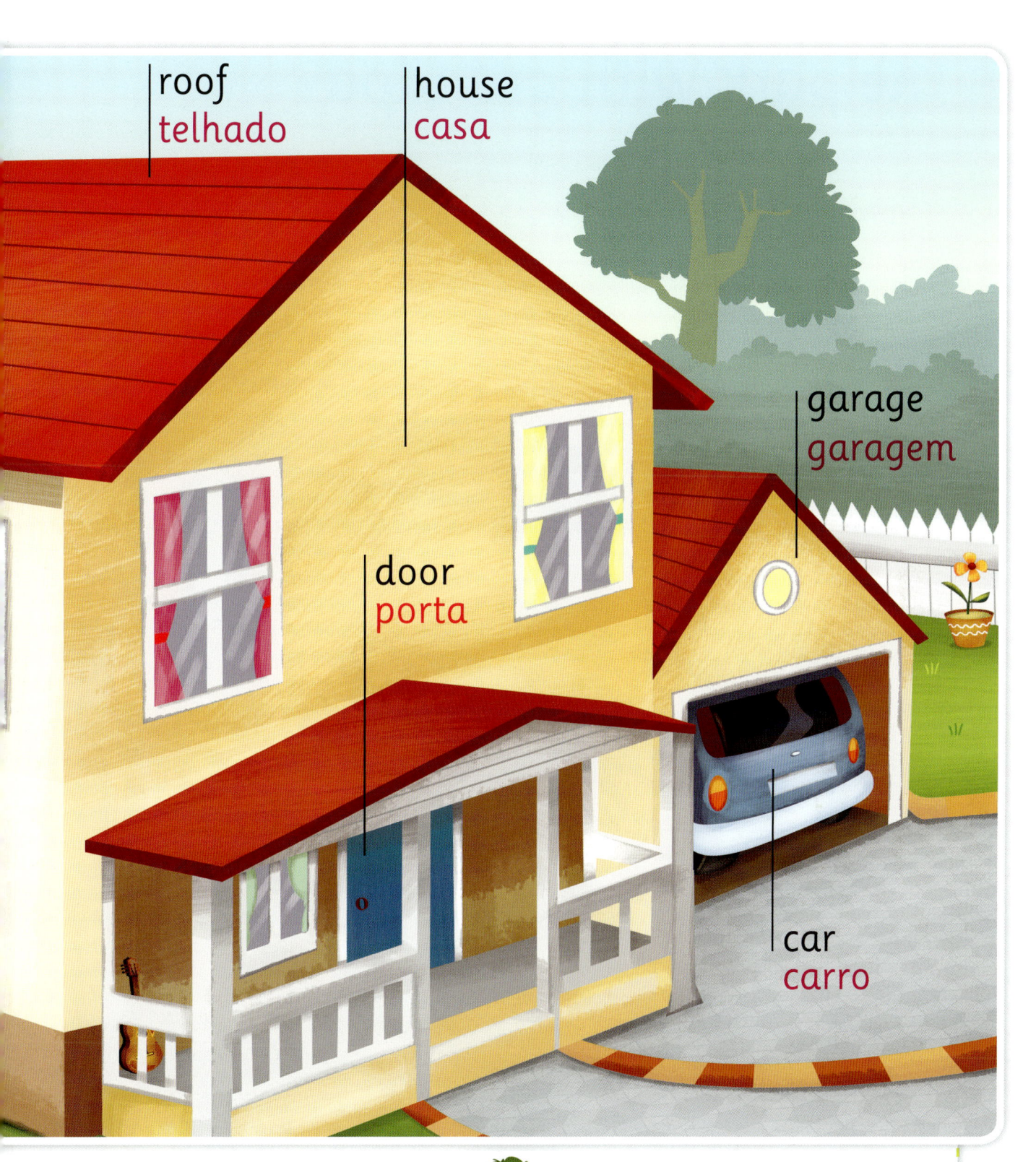

roof
telhado

house
casa

garage
garagem

door
porta

car
carro

Play in the garden
with the ball! (x 2)

Flowers and trees
around the house. (x 2)

Ben and Daisy run and
play. (x 2)

In the park with grandpa

boat
barco

lake
lago

kite
pipa

kick scooter
patinete

seesaw
gangorra

Activities

1. Find the hidden tortoise.
2. Sing the song!

Song

Swing, swing,
seesaw, slide!

ball
bola

climbing frame
trepa-trepa

bird
pássaro

swing
balanço

slide
escorregador

Row a boat,
fly a kite! (x 2)

In the park. (x 2)
In the park with grandpa!

In the park. (x 2)
In the park with grandpa!

Fairytale castle

prince
príncipe

jester
bobo da corte

princess
princesa

dragon
dragão

Activities

1. Find the hidden crab.
2. Sing the song!

Song

In this castle, oh, so big,

castle
castelo

knight
cavaleiro

minstrel
menestrel

king
rei

queen
rainha

live a princess and
a prince!

Happy minstrels play
a song,

for the king and
the queen!

Index